MW01109712

TRIBES of NATIVE AMERICA

Chickasaw

edited by Marla Felkins Ryan
and Linda Schmittroth

BLACKBIRCH®
PRESS

THOMSON
GALE

San Diego • Detroit • New York • San Francisco • Cleveland
New Haven, Conn. • Waterville, Maine • London • Munich

For more information, contact
The Gale Group, Inc.
27500 Drake Rd.
Farmington Hills, MI 48331-3535
Or you can visit our Internet site at http://www.gale.com

Photo credits: Cover Courtesy of Northwestern University Library; cover © National Archives; cover © Photospin; cover © Perry Jasper Photography; cover © Picturequest; cover © Seattle Post-Intelligencer Collection, Museum of History & Industry; cover © PhotoDisc; cover © Library of Congress; page 5 © Richard Hamilton Smith/Corbis; page 6, 7, 12, 13, 16–29 © Marilyn "Angel" Wynn / Nativestock.com; page 30 © NASA; page 14 © Medford Historical Society/Corbis; page 9 © The Art Archive/Gunshots; page 11 © Mary Evans Picture Library; page 8 © North Wind Picture Archive

LIBRARY OF CONGRESS CATALOGING-IN-PUBLICATION DATA

Chickasaw / Marla Felkins Ryan, book editor ; Linda Schmittroth, book editor.
    v. cm. — (Tribes of Native America)
Includes bibliographical references and index.
Contents: Name — History — Division over America's Civil War — Government — Current tribal issues.
  ISBN 1-56711-590-X (alk. paper)
  1. Chickasaw Indians—History—Juvenile literature. 2. Chickasaw Indians—Social life and customs—Juvenile literature. [1. Chickasaw Indians. 2. Indians of North America—Oklahoma.] I. Ryan, Marla Felkins. II. Schmittroth, Linda. III. Series.

  E99.C55C38 2003
  976.004'973—dc21

                    2003002626

Table of Contents

CHICKASAW

Name

Chickasaw (pronounced *CHICK-uh-saw*). The name comes from a story about two brothers, named Chisca and Chacta. The Chickasaw and Choctaw tribes are descended from these two men. English settlers called these Indians "Flat Heads."

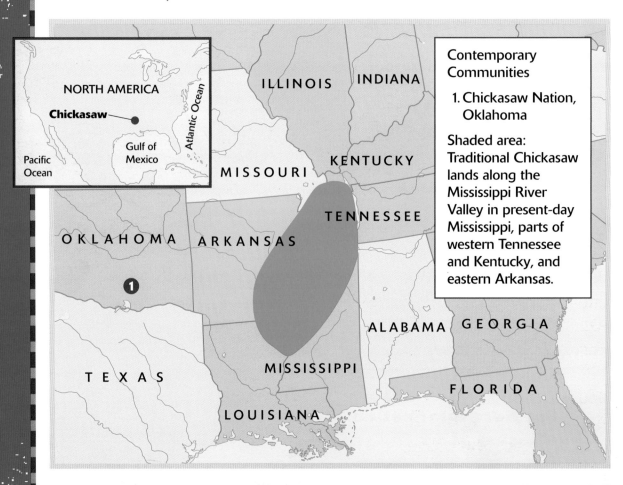

NORTH AMERICA

Chickasaw

Pacific Ocean

Gulf of Mexico

Atlantic Ocean

ILLINOIS   INDIANA

MISSOURI   KENTUCKY

OKLAHOMA   ARKANSAS   TENNESSEE

TEXAS   MISSISSIPPI   ALABAMA   GEORGIA

LOUISIANA   FLORIDA

Contemporary Communities

1. Chickasaw Nation, Oklahoma

Shaded area: Traditional Chickasaw lands along the Mississippi River Valley in present-day Mississippi, parts of western Tennessee and Kentucky, and eastern Arkansas.

Where are the traditional Chickasaw lands?

The Chickasaw lived in northeastern Mississippi near the Tombigbee River. They had plenty of food and land. The tribe controlled the Mississippi River valley. The Chickasaw also ruled parts of western Tennessee and Kentucky and eastern Arkansas. In 1723, state officials invited one group to settle in South Carolina along the Savannah River near Augusta, Georgia. By the end of the twentieth century, most Chickasaw lived in southern Oklahoma.

Traditional Chickasaw lands stretched across the Mississippi River valley.

What has happened to the population?

In 1693, there were about 10,000 Chickasaw. By 1890, there were 6,400. In a 1990 population count by the U.S. Bureau of the Census, 21,522 people said they were Chickasaw. This number is lower than the 35,000 members listed in the Chickasaw Nation. The Chickasaw tribe is the thirteenth largest Native American tribe in the United States.

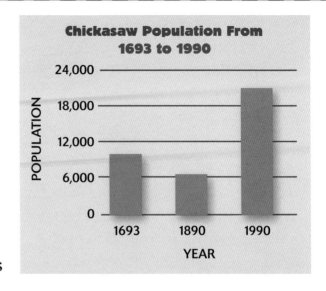

Chickasaw Population From 1693 to 1990

POPULATION

24,000
18,000
12,000
6,000
0

1693   1890   1990

YEAR

The Chickasaw people are the thirteenth-largest tribal nation in the United States. Many Chickasaw today maintain traditional tribal ways.

Origins and group ties

The Chickasaw were once part of the Choctaw tribe. Around 1300, the Chickasaw split from the Choctaw. The two tribes became enemies. The Chickasaw had few friends. They fought with nearly every tribe they met. The Chickasaw had battles with the Creek, Caddo, and Cherokee. They also fought with the Iroquois, Menominee, Potawatomi, and Shawnee.

The Chickasaw were fierce warriors. They frightened anyone who crossed their path. The British were impressed with the tribe's courage. The Chickasaw would take on any foe. They were not afraid when an enemy had a larger army. The British and Chickasaw became allies. The British traded weapons to the Chickasaw. Great Britain needed the tribe's help to win control of the North American continent. In the late 1700s, American colonists took over the eastern part of North America. The tribe was driven from its ancestral lands. The Chickasaw became part of a group known as the Five Civilized Tribes. These tribes were later forced to move to Oklahoma.

The Chickasaw and Choctaw were once members of the same tribe. In this illustration, Chickasaw and Choctaw men play a ball game.

HISTORY

Bad times with Spanish explorers

Long before the Europeans invaded the Mississippi River valley, the Chickasaw defended their lands against all newcomers. The tribe's lands had rich soil for crops, so many groups wanted to live there. Chickasaw men saw themselves first as warriors, then as hunters, and last as farmers.

In the winter of 1540, Spanish explorer Hernando de Soto led a group of men into Chickasaw territory. He was the first European to make contact with the tribe. The two groups did not trust each other. The Spanish demanded food and a place to set up their camp. Chief Miculasa unwillingly agreed. One day, the Spanish shared some of their

Hernando de Soto led a Spanish expedition into Chickasaw land in 1540.

roast pork with the tribe. The Chickasaw enjoyed the new dish. They began to take pigs from the Spanish group's herd. The Spanish killed two of the thieves. They cut off the hands of the third thief. Tensions grew between the Spanish and Chickasaw. The Chickasaw made a surprise attack on the Spanish and drove them off. The Spanish did not return.

Allies of the English

In 1700, English traders set up trading posts along the Mississippi River. The Chickasaw became their allies and trading partners. The traders had heard of the tribe's superior fighting skills. In exchange for animal skins and slaves, they gave the Chickasaw guns, tools, knives, and cotton cloth. The Chickasaw people began to use guns to hunt.

The English traded guns for animal skins and slaves with their Chickasaw allies.

1861
American Civil War begins

1865
Civil War ends

1869
Transcontinential Railroad is completed

1906
The Chickasaw Nation is dissolved

1917–1918
WWI fought in Europe

1929
Stock market crash begins the Great Depression

1941
Bombing at Pearl Harbor forces United States into WWII

1945
WWII ends

1970
The present-day Chickasaw Nation is granted the right to regroup and to elect its own leaders

1989–1990
The National Museum of the American Indian Act and the Native American Grave Protection and Reparations Act bring about the return of burial remains to native tribes

They also used their guns to attack the French. The French were in a battle with Spain and England for control of the North American continent.

To get more animal hides for trade, the Chickasaw began to hunt on the lands of their neighbors. They kidnapped the women and children of other tribes to trade as slaves. About this time, distant tribes were forced to move westward by American colonists. These uprooted tribes tried to take over Chickasaw land. Throughout the 1700s, the Chickasaw people engaged in almost constant fights.

The Chickasaw's contact with the English increased. The Chickasaw began to take on white ways. Many Chickasaw women married English men. These couples gave birth to children of mixed blood. The culture of the tribe was changed forever.

The Chickasaw were allies of the English until Great Britain's defeat in the American Revolution (1775–1783). After the war, the tribe signed a treaty with the Americans. Called the Treaty of Hopewell, this agreement set the borders of Chickasaw territory. American settlers were ordered to stay off this land.

Treaties reduce Chickasaw lands

In 1784, a measles outbreak struck the Chickasaw. It killed many of their leaders. The tribe was weak, but the Chickasaw still fought to defend their lands. The tribe began a battle with the Creek and Osage tribes.

These tribes had stolen from the Chickasaw and attacked their hunting parties. The war lasted for almost forty years.

The U.S. government told the Chickasaw and other tribes in the southern states that white settlers did not want their land. In time, the tribes lost trust in this promise. First, the Cherokee, Choctaw, and Creek tribes were forced to give up land to the U.S. government. Then, in 1801, the Chickasaw allowed Americans to build a road through their homeland. Within eight years, about five thousand whites settlers had moved illegally onto Chickasaw land.

In 1832, a treaty was signed that gave all Chickasaw lands east of the Mississippi River to the U.S. government. The Chickasaw were ordered to move to Indian Territory. This land forms most of

In the 1800s, the United States forced the Chickasaw off their lands. This illustration shows the Chickasaw battling the U.S. Army.

The Chickasaw were one of the group known as the Five Civilized Tribes. They are honored by the Five Civilized Tribes Museum in Muskogee, Oklahoma.

present-day Oklahoma. During the late 1800s, the U.S. government moved many tribes to Indian Territory. The government planned to make the area into a state governed by tribes.

The Chickasaw wanted their own land in Oklahoma. Tribe members searched but could not find land they liked. They finally decided to lease land from the Choctaw, their old enemies. The Chickasaw moved to Indian Territory with the Five Civilized Tribes. (The Five Civilized Tribes were the Chickasaw, Choctaw, Seminole, Creek, and Cherokee. White settlers gave the tribes this name because their habits were similar to those of whites.)

Move to Indian Territory

The five tribes took nearly twenty years to move to Indian Territory. The Chickasaw were the wealthiest of the five tribes. They had wagons, which made their move easier. The Chickasaw move took two years (1837–1838). Before the trip began, the tribe had 4,914

In 1855, under a treaty with the U.S. government, the Chickasaw were able to set up their own land boundaries. Pictured here are the Choctaw (left) and Chickasaw (below) sides of the boundary marker that separated them.

Chickasaw and 1,156 black slaves. The Chickasaw also took five thousand horses with them. Throughout the journey, many Chickasaw died from smallpox and a lack of food. Some died after they ate spoiled food given to them by the U.S. government.

Life in Indian Territory was hard. The region was filled with unhappy people from many different tribes. Some of these tribes were old enemies. The Chickasaw tribe began to live in Indian Territory on Choctaw land. The Chickasaw argued with each other and with the Choctaw. They feared the Choctaw might try to control them. This problem was solved in 1855. The Chickasaw signed a treaty with the U.S. government. This agreement set up the borders of an independent Chickasaw land. The next year, the Chickasaw people formed their nation.

Division over the Civil War

By 1856, the Chickasaw had come together as a tribe. Soon, though, their different political views began to divide the Chickasaw people again. Some members of the tribe were mixed-blood slaveholders. They had gained great wealth in American business. Others were traditional full-blooded Chickasaw. They were against slavery. When the Civil War began in 1861, many Chickasaw joined the Northern Union

During the Civil War, Native Americans in the Union Army (pictured) included many Chickasaw.

forces. They wanted to join the fight against slavery. At the same time, mixed-blood members of the official Chickasaw Nation signed a treaty with the Southern Confederacy.

After the war's end in 1865, white settlers began to move into Indian Territory. They ignored the laws that protected Indian lands. White settlers wanted changes made to the reservation system. They said that too much land was being set aside for Indians.

The breakup of Chickasaw lands

The Chickasaw were the wealthiest of the five nations that lived in Indian Territory. Yet, feuds often turned the Chickasaw against each other. These conflicts ended when the U.S. Congress started a new plan. The reservations were broken up into small plots of land. Each Indian was given a small plot of land to tend, called an allotment. Any leftover land was opened up to white settlement. This plan changed Chickasaw tradition. Before allotment, it had been the custom for the whole tribe to take care of large plots of land. The Chickasaw lands were divided up in 1897. Each full-blood Chickasaw was given 320 acres of land. Of the 6,319 members of the Chickasaw population, 1,535 members were full-blood.

In 1907, Oklahoma became the forty-sixth state. Shortly before this, the federal government broke up the Chickasaw Nation. By 1920, about three-fourths of Chickasaw lands had been either sold or leased to

The Chickasaw Nation was the wealthiest tribe in Indian Territory. Pictured here is the seal of the Chickasaw Nation.

whites. The Chickasaw Nation continued only as a tribal council. The council's governor was picked by the U.S. government.

Many Chickasaw people moved away or became part of the local population.

In 1970, Congress granted the Chickasaw tribe the right to elect its own leaders. The Chickasaw people were able to regroup. In the 1990s, the tribe began to recover from the loss of its lands to allotment.

As the twentieth century came to an end, most Chickasaw lived scattered throughout southern Oklahoma. There is a modern-day Chickasaw Nation, but the Chickasaw reservation no longer exists.

Religion

Everything in the Chickasaw world had religious meaning. The Chickasaw religion was closely tied to the moon and its phases. The Chickasaw believed in a supreme being called *Ababinili*. The tribe also believed in witches and evil spirits. In the old times, a priest called a *hopaye* led religious ceremonies. He explained to his followers the meaning of dreams and symbols.

The Chickasaw believed in a life after death. The good went to a world where they were rewarded for their life's work. The evildoers were trapped between the worlds. They were forced to wander in the Land of the Witches.

In the late 1800s, the Chickasaw learned of the Ghost Dance and Peyote (pronounced *pay-OH-tee*) religions. The Ghost Dance movement was started by a Paiute Indian named Wovoka. The religion told Indians to return to their traditional way of life. Followers believed that the Ghost Dance would bring their dead ancestors back to Earth. Life would be the way it was before white settlers arrived. The Peyote religion used the peyote cactus in its ceremonies. When eaten, peyote often produces visions. Followers of the Peyote religion believed these visions moved them closer to the spirit world.

In the Peyote religion, participants ate parts of the peyote cactus to have visions they felt were spiritual.

Pictured here is the Chickasaw Capitol Building in Tishomingo, Oklahoma.

Government

Traditional Chickasaw villages were independent. Only war could make the people forget their differences and unite. These villages were led by a chief, who inherited the job, and a war chief. Tribal elders and priests served as advisers.

After 1800, Chickasaw leaders allowed mixed-blood members of the tribe to oversee dealings with Americans. The mixed-bloods knew about the ways of the whites. Throughout the nineteenth century, they supported a government plan to give Chickasaw lands to white settlers. Some mixed-blood Chickasaw were paid by the U.S. government for their support of this plan.

In 1906, the U.S. government dissolved the Chickasaw Nation. The tribe was not happy with this action. The U.S. government began to pick tribal governors for the Chickasaw. In 1970, Congress granted the Chickasaw the right to elect their own tribal leadership. At that time, the Chickasaw elected Overton James as governor. His strong leadership created the modern Chickasaw Nation.

Economy

In traditional times, the Chickasaw were hunters who sometimes farmed. The arrival of the British changed the tribe's way of life. They began to trade heavily with the newcomers. Some mixed-blood Chickasaw began to run large plantations. They

In the 1970s and 1980s, the Chickasaw took out government loans to start businesses such as motels and restaurants.

The Chickasaw Nation's many businesses provide work for about thirteen hundred tribal members. Pictured here is the Chickasaw Nation Golf Course.

became very wealthy. They also used black slave labor.

Chickasaw life was upset by the tribe's move to Indian Territory. After some time passed, the Chickasaw began to prosper again. They became the wealthiest of the Five Civilized Tribes.

In the 1970s and 1980s, the Chickasaw used government loans to start their own businesses. These loans helped tribes to become less dependent on government help. Today, the Chickasaw Nation owns several gambling centers. These centers are a big source of money and jobs. About thirteen hundred people work for the Chickasaw Nation's many business. The nation has a motel, restaurant, a computer company, and trading posts.

DAILY LIFE

Families

Family lines are traced through the women of the Chickasaw tribe. Children usually take the name of their mother's house or clan. Men and women of the same house or clan name are not allowed to marry.

Buildings

Hundreds of years ago, Chickasaw families owned three buildings. Each family had a winter house, a summer house, and a storage building.

The winter house was dug three feet into the ground. Its frame was made from pine logs and poles. The wood frame was covered with clay for extra protection against the cold. A plaster made

Chickasaw children usually belong to their mother's clan.

Pictured here is a Chickasaw winter home.

from dried grasses was used to seal the cracks. These houses were very warm.

The Chickasaw summer house was rectangular in shape. Woven mats and clay plaster were used to build the walls. The roof was made of straw or tree bark. Summer houses had porches and balconies. A wall divided the inside of the house into two rooms. White pioneers of the West used this design as a model for their log cabins.

The size of Chickasaw villages depended on whether or not the tribe was at war. In times of peace, the villages were spread out from each other. In times of war, the houses and buildings were built more closely together. There were fewer villages, but each one had more homes in it. These larger villages were often built in the hills to discourage attackers.

White settlers copied the design of the Chickasaw summer house (pictured) for their homes.

Clothing

Chickasaw men were the tallest of any Native American tribe. Most were about six feet tall. Chickasaw women were about five feet tall. The Chickasaw had their heads flattened as babies. This was thought to be attractive. The British called the people "Flat Heads."

Chickasaw men wore breechcloths. These garments had front and back flaps that hung from the waist. In cold weather, men wore deerskin shirts, robes of bear fur, and deerskin boots. For special ceremonies or to prepare for war, men painted their faces. The bravest warriors wore capes made from swan feathers. Chickasaw men shaved the hair along the sides of their heads. The tuft of hair left down the center was kept in place with bear grease. Chickasaw women simply tied up their long hair. They wore dresses made of deerskin.

The Chickasaw hunted deer for its meat and skin. Both men and women wore clothing made of deerskin.

Food

In traditional Chickasaw life, the men hunted and the women grew crops and gathered food. The men of the tribe were excellent animal trackers and trappers. They used animal calls and decoys to lure wild game such as deer, buffalo, and bear. Fish were

In addition to meat, fish, and nuts, the Chickasaw ate fruit that was grown and dried by the women.

lured out of deep waters with poisoned nuts, then easily speared or caught in a net.

The women grew many wild foods. Favorite foods were strawberries, persimmons, onions, honey, and nuts. They also dried fruit and made tea from wild roots and herbs.

Education

At birth, infant boys were placed on a panther skin. The Chickasaw believed the baby would gain the animal's fierceness and power. This ritual began their training as warriors. Male children were trained by their mother's brothers.

Healing practices

The Chickasaw believed that evil spirits caused sickness. Traditional Chickasaw healers, called *aliktce,* fought these spirits with potions and teas. In the Picofa Ceremony, healers performed special rituals over a sick person for three days. During this

Healers used ritual tools to heal fellow Chickasaw. Pictured here is a medicine rattle made from a turtle foot.

time, a fire was kept before the victim's front door. The fire faced east, opposite the Land of the Dead. Family members of the sick person danced around the fire at night. The name *Picofa* comes from the cracked corn and pork dish that was eaten on the final day of the ceremony.

Literature

Like many other tribes, the Chickasaw told tales about great floods that ended the world. The Chickasaw also had creation stories. These stories told of their travels from the Far West to the New World in ancient times. According to tribal lore, the Choctaw and the Chickasaw moved over a long period of time, not all at once. At that time, they were part of one tribe known as the Chickemacaw. The tribe followed two brothers, Chisca and Chacta. The brothers carried a magical pole that leaned toward the East. This pole showed the people where to settle on the eastern side of the Mississippi River.

CUSTOMS

Festivals, games, and ceremonies

Like the Seminole and other southern tribes, Chickasaw men took part in a ceremony in which they swallowed a strong black drink. The potion made them vomit. This was meant to purify them. In the summer, Chickasaw men played a violent form of football. The games lasted a full day and involved hundreds of players.

The Chickasaw have two major festivals each year. One is called the Renewal of Traditions. The festival lasts for two days in July. It includes the Stomp Dance, ball games, storytelling, and traditional foods and crafts. The Chickasaw Festival and Annual Meeting lasts for one week. It is held each September. The festival has a princess pageant, Chickasaw Nation Junior Olympics, and a powwow.

The Stomp Dance is part of the Renewal of Traditions festival that the Chickasaw hold in July.

A traditional Chickasaw ball game using equipment like that shown here is played during the July festival.

War and hunting rituals

Chickasaw war parties were small. Each had about thirty to fifty men. The warriors were best known for sneak attacks on their enemies. Even after they got horses, Chickasaw warriors often traveled on foot because their lands were heavily wooded.

The Chickasaw believed that the ghost of a dead warrior would haunt his family until the person who killed him was punished. Often, the widows of warriors killed in battle slept on the graves of their dead husbands.

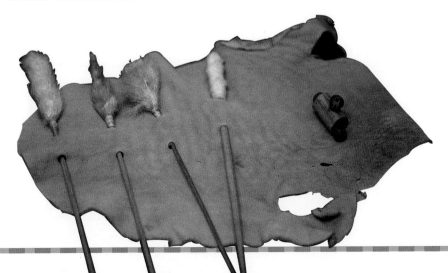

The Chickasaw, like many other Native American people, used blowguns and darts (pictured) for hunting.

Chickasaw men proposed by offering cloth for a dress. Here, modern Chickasaw women wear traditional dresses.

Courtship and marriage

Women set up marriages in the Chickasaw tribe. If a man wanted to marry, he sent his mother or sister to the chosen girl's family. His relative took with her enough cloth to make at least one dress. If the girl's family agreed to the proposal, the bundle of cloth was offered to the bride-to-be. The girl agreed to the marriage if she accepted the material. Then, a wedding ceremony was held.

When a Chickasaw man married a woman, he also took on her sisters. He could choose to live with all of them. When a man died, his brother had the right to marry his widow.

Funerals

When they died, the Chickasaw were buried beneath their houses. They were often buried with their belongings. The faces of the dead were painted red. Their bodies were placed in a sitting position to face west. The tribe believed that the land of the afterlife lay to the west.

Current tribal issues

By the end of the twentieth century, the landless Chickasaw Nation began to become more self-sufficient. The tribe wants to end the U.S. government's involvement in its affairs. The Chickasaw work hard to provide jobs for their people and to educate their children.

The headquarters of the Chickasaw Nation are located in Ada, Oklahoma.

John Herrington (inset) became the first Native American in space in 2002.

Notable people

John Herrington (1958–) is an astronaut who on November 23, 2002 became the first Native American in space. Linda Hogan (1947–) is a professor of Native American Studies. She is also is a writer and poet. Her poems and stories are about Chickasaw life. Other notable Chickasaw include the writer and educator Geary Hobson (1941–). He is a strong supporter of Native American writing. Towana Spivey (1943–) is an anthropologist and museum curator.

For more information

Official Web site of the Chickasaw Nation
http://www.chickasaw.net

Sultzmann, Lee. *Chickasaw History.*
http://dickshovel.com/chick.html. Sumners, Cecil L. *The True Story of Chief Tishomingo.* Amory, MS: Amory Advertiser, 1974.

Glossary

Hopaye a Chickasaw priest

Ghost Dance a religion that promised Native Americans a return to their old way of life

Peyote religion a Native American religion that included the use of peyote, a cactus that produces visions when eaten

Powwow a Native American gathering or ceremony

Reservation land set aside for Native Americans by the government

Treaty an agreement between two or more parties

Index